Why You will NOT Die

A science-based argument that Death does Not exist

By Robert Marino

Researched 2006 - 2020

Dedication

In Darwinian terms, I have survived thanks to the birth of my children.

Ann, Jane, Mary and Olivia, through the miraculous process of birth you have completed me. The half of my genes NOT used to create you was filtered out so that you have achieved a brilliance and beauty that I never could. Only the necessities of gathering resources for you have kept me from the one thing I truly desire - spending every moment in your company. The bond I have for you has revealed to me a new, eternal dimension of life. It exists in a place fulfilled. I love you.

Introduction

Life on our planet has adapted to live in hospitable places like Florida, fresh and salt water, and less inviting places like the Antarctic, thermal fissures, sulfur pools (extremophiles) and other diverse environs. Given that life is so virile and adaptive, why does it succumb to death just because it has lived? This question caused me to go on a decade long search for the answer only to find out it was a false question caused by mankind's ego. **Death does not exist. It is folklore**. This is NOT a paper about religion. It relies only on facts, data, and scientific research. No preaching here. Skepticism will come. Good, it will shine light/insight onto the subject so bring it on! Until a dead person comes forward to set us all straight...oh wait, that's the issue isn't it?

Before I argue why death does not exist, I will first describe what causes what we now view as death. To do that I will use the term death until we are ready to redefine it.

What is Killing You?

Aging is just a friendlier term for dying, so even if we don't expire immediately after the birth of our child we are still dying. Yet we are surrounded by life that doesn't die just because it has aged. All of life's ancestors were single cell organisms, and they were and are ageless.

These life forms are known as prokaryotes. Prokaryotes appeared four billion years ago and are the earliest known life on this planet. Their DNA is very different from ours. While our DNA is in the form of a double helix (eukaryotic), prokaryotes have circular DNA (a ring). This difference is critical to aging and our view of death.

Eukaryotes, a class of organism that now includes multicellular humans and single cell paramecia, appeared on earth 2 billion years ago. Unlike the life that preceded them, Eukaryotes were/are subject to the **Hayflick Limit,** a limit on the life forming potential of our cells because each cell division uses up a precious part of the cell. In 1961, Leonard Hayflick and Paul Moorhead demonstrated that human cells can only divide a limited amount of times in culture (Hayflick & Moorhead, 1961). This finite potential is now known as the "Hayflick Limit". While its function is not completely understood, an enzyme called telomerase helps regulate aging. Telomerase, a ribonucleic acid, is found near the end of chromosomes. It serves to synthesize the ends of chromosomes known as the telomeric DNA. Telomeres (TM) are DNA sequences which maintain the fidelity of genetic information during cellular division. The telomeres become shorter after each cell division. Once a telomere (TM) reaches a critical length shortage, the cell that hosts it is no longer capable of dividing and forming a viable "daughter" cell. **The amount of TM at the end of these genes will determine the amount of life this cell will spawn by governing the total number of times this cell can divide.** When a cell divides in an adult, half of the TM goes with the new cell and half of the TM stays with the original cell. Life is at death's doorstep once the TM becomes too short to sustain cellular division. For mankind, young adults begin with enough TM to allow each cell (expect gametes) to divide and form new cells (new life) approximately 50 times. After that comes what we know as death.

Multicellular organisms start as a single cell organism, the fertilized egg. At this stage of life and for the growth phase afterward, our cells behave more like those of single cell organisms. During this time, telomerase activity is high and TM length is maintained. If not, the lifespan of our species would be ridiculously short, and humans could only reach an age and size of 50 cells. Instead, the growing years of an organism operate with a completely different set of rules. Paramecia, found a way past this TM shortening issue and how they do so set an evolutionary path for us and all other eukaryotes to avoid extinction due to aging (more on that in a bit). Stem cells (first cells of new life) are like paramecia in that they can reset the Hayflick Limit in response to being near-senescent. During this phase, organisms can replenish TM.

Algae (pond scum) is a close relative to the origin of life on this planet. As a single cell prokaryote, it did not follow the rules of TM reduction that kills eukaryotes and the adults of multicellular species. If it were vulnerable to TM shortening, the bacterium would simply run out of TM and become extinct and we wouldn't need antibacterial soap. Instead, they continue to divide, follow an ancient genetic path and grow new cells in an endless chain, occasionally taking the time to mutate and start new endless chains along the way. One of those new paths included the mutation that produced the first single cell eukaryote and eventually us.

Single cell eukaryotes such as paramecia had a problem. They needed a means to overcome the Hayflick Limit to survive. If not, as paramecia reached the Hayflick Limit they and their progeny would be at death's doorstep and the entire species would face extinction. To survive, paramecia had to develop another method of reproduction. Single cell eukaryotes normally reproduce through mitosis (cell division). This method of reproduction depletes the Hayflick Limit, which is approximately 200 cell divisions for this species. As paramecium reach 200 divisions, they begin to expire. Since mitosis produces an exact genetic replication of the mother cell, the progeny of aged paramecia, would be two identical daughter cells at the same advanced age and ready to expire as well. Clearly this would leave paramecia on the verge of extinction.

To overcome this limitation, these organisms employ a second method of reproduction. This method, known as conjugation, requires genes from two different aged individuals, each swapping half its genes with the other, like sexual reproduction. Conjugation resets the biological clock back to a potential of 200 cell divisions for the individuals involved. The old paramecia are now genetically different (each now having half the genes from the other) and they become young again. They have become their own children.

The paramecia possess two nuclei, the micronucleus and macronucleus. The micronucleus of the paramecium starts as diploid and is used to support the conjugative reproduction. Once the paramecium reaches its Hayflick Limit, the micronucleus divides and exchanges half its genes with another. This exchange resets the Hayflick Limit back to its original potential. It also allows for successful new traits (mutations) to be passed on. More on that in a bit.

The macronuclei of paramecium contain reserves of DNA and are beyond diploid. These reserves are slowly depleted with each cellular division. A new macronucleus is formed through conjugative reproduction, while the old macronucleus is ejected, withers and disintegrates. The paramecium differentiated a portion of the cell (the micronucleus) for reproduction and a portion for resources to "nurture" cellular activity (the macronucleus). By sharing DNA with another of the same species, genetic improvements (mutations that withstood the test of natural selection) could be shared with the balance of the community's future generations. However, the portion of the cell containing the old genetic information (the macronucleus) was destroyed and replaced in the process. **This step would evolve and establish aging and what we view as death in all multicellular organisms to come.**

What Defines Life Expectancy?

In Darwinian terms, you have survived once you have passed your genes into the genepool. If you expire due to cancer the next day, you have still survived. The most callous example of Darwinian survival that I could find is this: The Mayfly lives for just one day after maturing from larva to fly. Some species of Mayfly expire in just five minutes, yet they are not extinct. The mayfly's mouth doesn't work due to mutation. It can't eat.

This causes the mayfly to expire quickly after reaching the adult stage of its life cycle. During its limited time, it mates so that the species may continue. This mutation survived because it doesn't affect mayfly individuals until after they have passed their genes into the genepool. It's all very mechanical.

The mechanics also worked to create freakishly long-lived, cave dwelling crayfish, which exist nowhere else on earth but one Floridian cave. These creatures reach an age of at least 100 years (the study continues). Have these freakishly long-lived crayfish found the fountain of youth right where Ponce de Leon had believed it to be?

Similar, long-lived but different species of crayfish have now been found in other caves in the American southeast. These creatures, which live in a unique and very finite environment, are genetic oddities since they somehow developed the ability to astronomically outlive their terrestrial cousins who by comparison only live an average of 2 – 3 years.

This photo is courtesy of www.sherpaguides.com

The cave dwelling crayfish started off as genetically identical to their terrestrial cousins as they entered the cave. They lost their pigment over the millenniums due to the cave's total darkness. Total darkness also made eyes useless, and they too were removed by evolution. As these traits receded, another trait became dominant for the mating game.

Here, in this Floridian cave, was an environment where the gene pool would favor greater longevity.

Reproductive Influences on Lifespan: A species' reproductive profile impacts lifespan. Greater lifespan provides the individual more opportunities to procreate than a short-lived individual thereby allowing greater contribution for long-lived genes into the gene pool. Those individuals with greater lifespan, due to slight genetic variances, have great impact to the cave's limited gene pool because total population is small. The competition for resources in a small environment, with a limited number of competitors, hastens evolution just as it did for the birds, tortoises and iguanas of the Galapagos. Above ground, there is less competition for space and other resources.

Over the millenniums of time this environment yielded a new long-lived species of crayfish and provided **strong evidence that a relationship between reproduction and lifespan** exists. These cave dwelling crayfish don't even reach sexual maturity until age 40, long after their terrestrial cousins have died. Sexually mature, younger males would be a threat to the alpha male. Delaying sexual maturity would improve the chances for a male of the next generation to one-day overthrow the alpha male. Reproductive norms have also influenced human lifespan.

A person who possesses an abnormally long lifespan does not know that when he/she has children. A couples' lifespan potential was not a determining factor in their mating. We are compelled by our genes and now culture to survive and procreate. Societal pressures also serve to dissuade us from having children very late in life. The act of having children early in life retards our species' lifespan.

Our current genetic-driven (in the sense that genes dictate organs that will manufacture hormones) sex drive is a basic Darwinian survival strategy. We have children – the species survives. **Having children therefore ensures our survival as a species but, as you are about to see, also ensures our timely death as individuals**. Our culture has contributed to our current lifespan because young adults have children. This is the way the game is played currently. If the rules of the mating game were realigned to reward long life, the lifespan potential of humans would begin to increase; driven by our gene pool and not better nutrition and medicine, though that helps our life expectancy.

If it were NOT permissible to have children until later than customary in life, the gene pool would begin to be influenced by the trait of living longer. I don't recommend this practice and given our sex drive, a strong strategy for survival, I do not believe it could be enforced. **Longer human lifespan would evolve if our species' parents would delay and/or prolong their child producing years.** For example, if a law were passed to create a minimum age for parents (MAP) that disallowed anyone under the age of 38 to have children, a large number of individuals would expire before they ever had the opportunity to become parents. Only those couples that could live that long and stay fertile that long would be able to have children. This would filter out those that succumb to disease and those that could not maintain fertility until they reached the MAP. If in five years after the law was enacted the MAP was increased to 39, and five years after increased to 40 and so on, several interesting traits would emerge.

The population size would first rapidly decrease as those that didn't survive or couldn't stay fertile until the MAP would fail to have children and these "inferior" genes would no longer be contributed to the genepool. That opens the door for long-lived and fertile individuals to overwhelm the gene pool with their contribution to it in the form of their progeny. While this was happening, the average age of puberty would also begin to rise. Mankind would also begin to change its size. First, the average height would drop and then eventually grow beyond our present stature and keep growing for as long as the MAP is manipulated. This link to size will be described later. Finally, the lifespan of humans would increase and keep increasing until the law was banned. If this was carried out for generations, the lifespan of mankind would leap forward just as it did for the cave dwelling crayfish and the Galapagos tortoises. Can crazy approaches like this really work? Yes, they can and have already.

Eggs are present in the female at birth and they never divide (until fertilized) and therefore are never exposed to the shortening of telomeres, which results from cell division in an adult. Sperm cells are the result of cell divisions, yet unlike other cells, their telomere lengthens as the male ages. More aged fathers at conception therefore positively impacts the life expectancy of the child. Natural selection, as it always does, has found a way to respond to the environment. An environment where fathering occurs at later ages requires offspring to live longer so they can do the same; (*Older paternal ages and grandpaternal ages at conception predict longer telomeres in human descendants* published May 19, 2019 by Royal) Society https://royalsocietypublishing.org/doi/10.1098/rspb.2019.0800.

Green sea turtles (turtles live most of their life in the water while tortoises spend most of their time on land) match a great size with great longevity. Living up to 80 years and growing to great size, they have developed some unique survival strategies.

Every couple of years, the females of the species, beach themselves and lay over one hundred eggs. When the hatchlings emerge, most die. The mother is not there to protect the offspring from the predatory birds, which massacre most of the hatchlings, as they attempt to reach the relative safety of the water. They must lay many eggs to improve the chances that some make it to the water, complete the cycle, of life and ensure the survival of this species. The greater the number of eggs in the nest, the better the chance for survival. Thus, individuals that lay more eggs than average will contribute this trait to the gene pool at a higher rate than normal. Over thousands of years, all the females of the species became prolific egg layers.

The gene pool of the sea turtle community is not only influenced by the number of eggs per nest but also by the total number of nests mothers produce in their lifetime. Those turtles that live longer get the opportunity to make more nests. Since sea turtles continue to produce offspring throughout their adult life (very unlike humans), the length of their lives allows long-lived sea turtles to contribute more than others to the species' gene pool. This greater contribution slowly influences the gene pool more and more, eventually increasing the lifespan and therefore number of nests/eggs for the entire species. Long-lived, prolific egg layers contribute more to the specie's gene pool than others. This combination greater number of eggs per nest, along with a higher than average number of reproductive years has caused sea turtles to evolve and increase the lifespan of the species.

Species

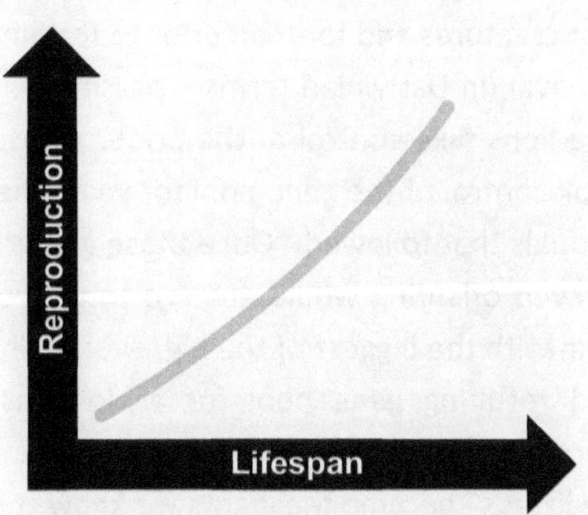

Humans who live long tend to NOT influence the gene pool any more or less than short-lived individuals because they stop having children earlier in life and therefore, they contribute no more or less to the gene pool than short-lived individuals.   Other species continue to reproduce throughout their life. Unlike modern humans, these species have a strong correlation between sexual reproduction and lifespan. Creatures with more prolific procreation tendencies have a greater lifespan than creatures with less prolific procreation tendencies. The mayfly reproduces once before it dies of starvation. If a mutation occurs that would allow one mayfly to eat and therefore live long enough to give rise to a second litter, the gene pool of this mayfly species will eventually share this successful trait to all members of the species, thereby increasing the lifespan of the species solely due to an increase in reproductive capacity. **Species that possess the ability to reproduce rapidly or in great number throughout their life will tend to live longer than species (of the same size) that possess less prolific reproduction capacity.**

The Relationship of Size to Lifespan: For increased lifespan, it is a privileged position to be a member of a large-bodied species. Large creatures in general live longer than small creatures. The Dinosaurs were gargantuan. Why? Most members of a species seem to be attracted to large alpha males and females (queen bee, queen aunt, the male lion, etc.). This is not an accident. This tendency provides advantages for survival. For most creatures and for man prior to forming civilization, size was critical to survival (in Darwinian terms – passing genes into the gene pool). Large male lions take control of the pride. Those that were large and lived long took control of the gene pool for years thereby shaping the pool for all individuals that followed. Once those genes were in the gene pool, large, long-lived offspring would emerge to play out the battle for survival once again with the biggest of the big, eventually claiming control of the pride and resulting gene pool for as long as they can. For dinosaurs, this process was repeated for hundreds of millions of years until the "terrible lizards" became the giants we know them to have been. This species enlarging process continues but less so in the mammalian world, since unlike reptiles and crustaceans, mammals don't continue to grow throughout their lives. Humans have now adopted a mostly monogamous culture, thereby interrupting the process of slowly growing our species' size.

An increase of our stature would normally also allow for the evolutionary increase of our lifespan. However, mankind's modern mating practices no longer reward the gene pool more richly by those individuals that possess the ability to live long, grow large and continue to procreate late into life. The result is that our lifespan remains unchanging or at least less changing than would have otherwise been the case. Before our culture produced military, police and fire departments, our ancestors relied on large, powerful males for protection. Written in our genes, most women are attracted to tall, muscular men. There is little doubt that these attributes stem from an age when the protection of the clan from physical harm was more directly the responsibility of the patriarch. Given that smaller males live longer (why will be described next), and security issues are now addressed well by our government and security alarms, perhaps women should begin to favor petite men so as to provide greater longevity to their children. Nature, however, is not so easily overridden.

A **species** will tend to increase its stature as its lifespan increases. The increased size prolongs the growth phase of life while providing enough TM potential to support the balance of life in the dying phase. The strong correlation between size and lifespan is easy to see. Creatures such as whales live long. Whales can reach an age of at least 200 years. The size of shark species correlates strongly to lifespan. The larger the shark species, the longer the lifespan. Whale sharks, which can reach a length of 60 feet, live between 100 – 150 years old. While 10 feet varieties live just 10 -15 years. As their name indicates, great white sharks are large and assumed to live between 40 – 50 years (there must be some joke about not knowing for sure because they tend to eat the researchers before the study is completed).

Land creatures roughly follow a similar size/lifespan correlation. Mice (2 years) are survived by dogs (12 – 15 years), which are survived by lions (20 years), which are survived by horses (25 – 30 years), which are survived by elephants (60 – 70 years). Why?

Species

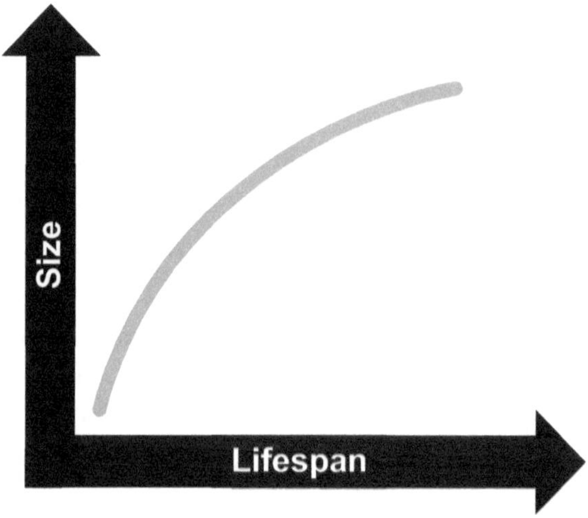

It takes time to grow to gargantuan size. To accomplish this, the species must maintain their TM, as it is consumed by the cell division necessary to achieve great size. This delays the transition from the growth phase to the dying phase plus leaves these larger species with enough residual telomerase to complete their life. Therefore, larger species normally possess a longer lifespan than smaller species.

The Giants Among Us are Close to Immortal: Giants such as whales live long but just roughly as long as sea tortoises because the latter species make up for their size disadvantage with reproductive proliferation that the whale lacks. Creatures that possess both the trait for prolific reproduction and great size should yield the greatest lifespan. Giant creatures with great reproduction ability are hard to hide. Just look up.

The redwood tree is the largest known organism on earth. Some specimens weigh 1.6 million pounds and reach a height of 150 meters. Most amazing of all, is the staggering age. Some individuals are 2000 years old and fossil evidence promotes the belief that they can reach an age of 4000 years old. Wow! Redwood trees have a more stable version of telomerase than most creatures. The telomerase found in this species is cross-linked (chained together) to provide stability for centuries of telomere replenishment.

Lifespan

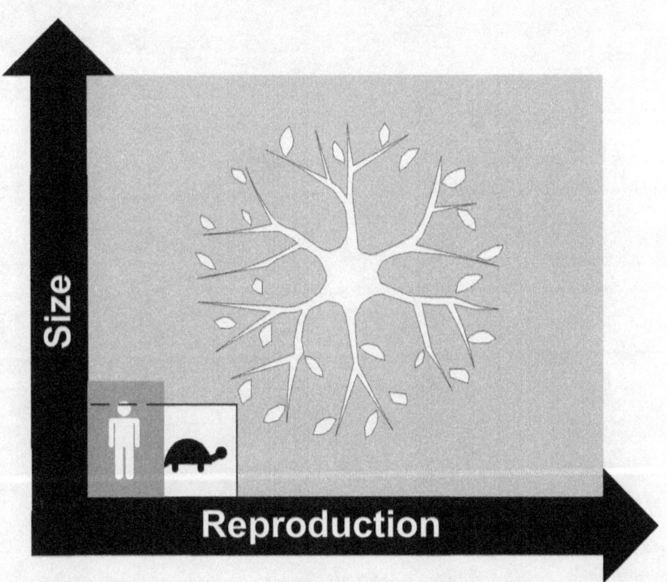

The illustration above uses a shaded region instead of the trend lines of previous illustrations to depict lifespan. Larger areas therefore equate to a longer lifespan. By comparing the size and reproductive differences between species the relative lifespan of each can be measured.

Elephants have a lifespan very similar to humans despite their superior size. However, elephant gestation is three times longer than humans and therefore limits the number of offspring produced in its lifetime, slowing the impact upon the elephant gene pool by longer-lived individuals. Humans may have more offspring than elephants, but elephants grow larger. Thus, the result is two different sized species with a similar lifespan.

The ability to keep growing also influences lifespan: The hydra seems to be near immortal. This ancient life form lives in fresh water and resembles an anemone. It can be starved to death or killed but it doesn't seem to age. It can also grow back severed appendages. In fact, it can be cut into many pieces and each piece will grow into another full hydra.

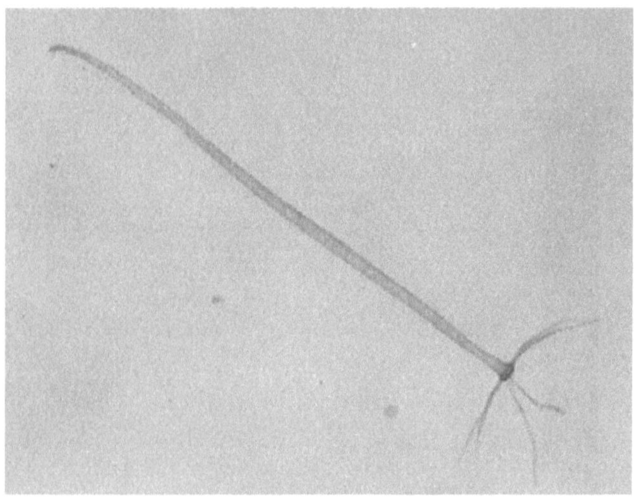

Hydra

Mankind is not vulnerable to the Hayflick Limit while we grow as evidenced by our growth from a fertilized egg beyond our Hayflick Limit of 50 cell divisions. While growing we are not dying because we are replenishing TM. The hydra's genetic aptitude to re-grow its body maintains its life suspended within the growth phase. In this phase, the TM lost in cellular division is restored. Creatures that possess regeneration also possess the great lifespan.

Another example of the correlation of growth and aging come from researchers at the University of Nottingham have demonstrated how a species of flatworm overcomes the aging process to be potentially immortal.

"Planarian worms have amazed scientists with their apparently limitless ability to regenerate. Researchers have been studying their ability to replace aged or damaged tissues and cells in a bid to understand the mechanisms underlying their longevity." The worms' ability to stay in the growth phase of life pushes back aging/dying.

The Individual's Size Impacts Life Expectancy: It is an even greater privilege to be a small individual of that species. On average, smaller individuals enjoy greater life expectancy than larger individuals of the same species. Larger individuals are comprised of more cells. Those who suffer gigantism and even tall, large individuals are on average prone to an earlier death than smaller individuals. TM is a precious commodity that supports both growth and longevity. The cell division required for the greater number of cells in a large individual consumes this precious commodity for life at a more rapid rate compared to smaller individuals within the same species.

Individuals within a Species

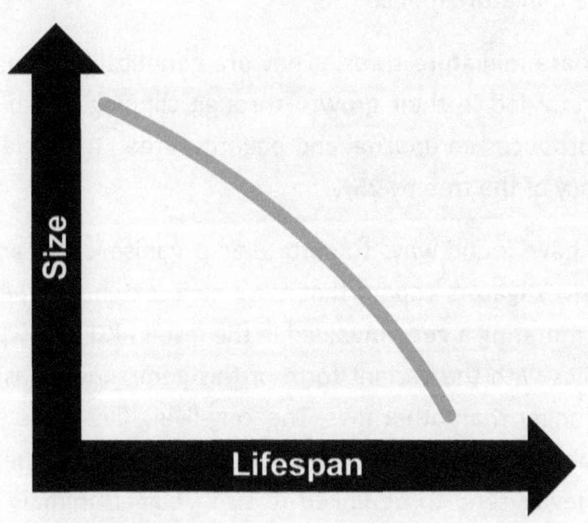

The individual/size relationship is remarkably apparent in dog breeds. Great Danes (7 - 10 years) are survived by German Shepherds (10 - 12

years) which are survived by terriers (12 - 14 years) which are survived by poodles (13 - 15 years) which are survived by Chihuahuas (14 - 20 years).

Miniature mice, a naturally occurring mutation, are conceived with the normal telomerase potential of their species, yet their individual genetic variation for smaller size requires less telomerase to support their growth phase. This allows for more telomere potential to be carried forward into this individual's death phase thus serving to prolong life. Normal mice live to an average age of 2 years. Mini-mice consistently live 50% to 100% longer, some reaching an age of over 4 years.

Miniature horses are the same species as Arabian and Clydesdale and all other breeds of horses. This means that they can be successfully mated with any other breed of horse. They have been selectively bred to yield a miniature stature. Horses of customary size have an average life expectancy of between 25 and 30 years. Miniature horses do not have a "miniature" life expectancy. They live to be 50 years old for the same reason as the miniature mouse.

Bonsai trees are miniature trees. They are genetically normal trees that have been retarded in their growth through clipping and binding. This ancient art produces an unusual and beautiful tree. It also lengthens the life expectancy of the tree by 25%.

Researchers have found ways to mutate an organism's size and therefore lifespan. "Investigators report that they have extended the lifespan of fruit flies by mutating a gene involved in the insulin-IGF (growth hormone) pathway. Flies with the variant form of this gene, known as chico, lived nearly 50% longer than other flies. The long-living flies were smaller than average, probably due to decreased IGF levels. In mammals, including people, IGF levels tend to be linked to size - bigger animals have higher levels of the growth factor". Science, April 6, 2001; 292:104-110.

The preceding examples show that that the small kid, picked last at recess, will have the last laugh.

Life Expectancy and Size of Race

Thanks to America's melting pot, data now exists to prove the link between the size of races and life expectancy. By studying various races living in America, we can filter out environmental differences that exist in their homelands and examine more directly the correlation of race size/life expectancy.

The following chart portrays the average life expectancy of citizens of 16 nations. The 2003 data is listed in descending order and supplied by the website of the Central Intelligence Agency (CIA) of the US government. Viewed in this form, no strong correlation between size and longevity is visible. This is either because no correlation exists or because there are differences in the standards of living and other environmental factors between these nations. These differences may impact the life expectancy of their citizens and obscure any correlation between size and longevity that may exist. It will be necessary to filter out these environmental factors to determine the answer.

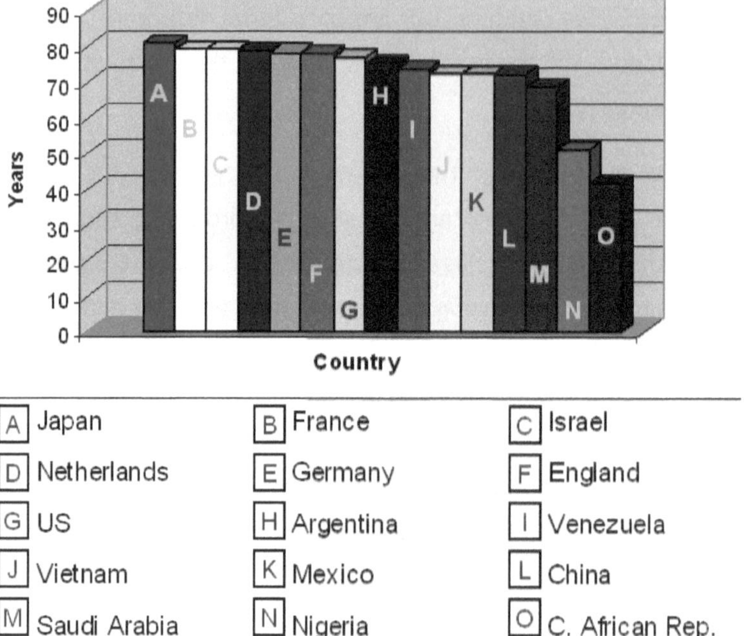

A	Japan	B	France	C	Israel
D	Netherlands	E	Germany	F	England
G	US	H	Argentina	I	Venezuela
J	Vietnam	K	Mexico	L	China
M	Saudi Arabia	N	Nigeria	O	C. African Rep.

Asian nations are found at both ends of the spectrum while European nations enjoy consistent longevity. African and Hispanic nations have consistently poor life expectancy. The vast majority of the diverse life expectancy shown in this chart is due to differences in wealth, nutrition, environment and healthcare and not genetics. Again, Asian nations are found on both ends of the chart.

The US (the melting pot) has an abundance of citizens of all races. By studying the resulting life expectancy of races living in the US (therefore filtering out as best we can the influences of nutrition and healthcare) we should be better able to illustrate that the size of the race has a direct correlation to that race's lifespan. Due to the diversity of environments the US has to offer, it would also be meaningful to examine data for different races living in the same state to minimize the impact of environmental influences.

The following graph very strongly demonstrates the relationship of size and life expectancy in humans by studying four races living in California.

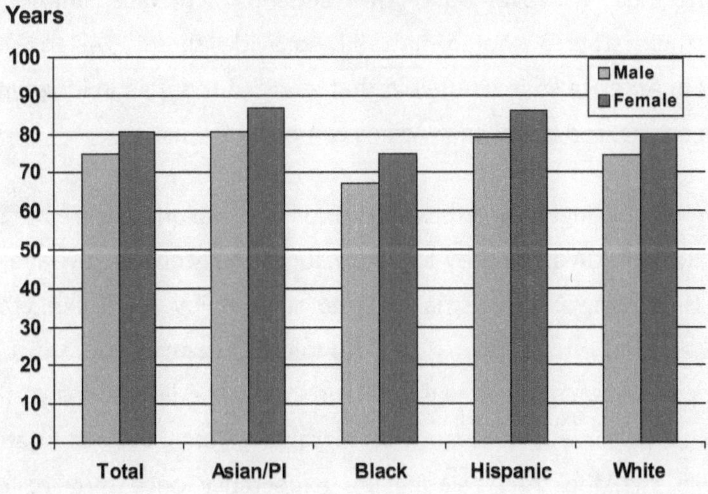

CENTER FOR HEALTH STATISTICS
DATA MATTERS
REPORT REGISTER NO. DM99-10000

Fortunately, minorities living in CA enjoy life expectancy that is improved compared to that of their native lands. Blacks, which are the largest race (stature) living in the US, have the lowest life expectancy. Perhaps this is not surprising given the relatively poor life expectancy found in African nations. Furthermore, Blacks unfortunately on average receive lower than average salaries and therefore may lack the economic resources for access to the best healthcare.

Caucasians living in CA have a similar (comparatively long by international standards) life expectancy to that of European nations.

Life expectancy of Asians living in CA soars past the life expectancy of whites as well as that found in most of their native lands. Proof that once the limitations of nutrition and healthcare confronting Asians in some of their homelands are overcome, this small-framed race enjoys the longevity their stature should naturally provide them.   Asians have prospered in America so it is possible that some of this gain in longevity is due to the specialized healthcare Asians can now afford.

The claim of privileged healthcare cannot be reasonably credited to Hispanics living in CA since they too unfortunately receive below average income. Hispanics, another small-framed race, enjoy a life expectancy greater than that of whites. They completely reverse the short life expectancy experienced in their homelands once the limitations of their native nations are overcome. Immigrants from various nations dramatically changed their relative life expectancy once they become residents of America.

The Mechanics Governing Life

Multicellular eukaryotes have a gene pool because mothers and fathers evolved as well. Mutations are passed into this gene pool, and if they stand the test of time through natural selection they can become part of the species survival strategy. Prokaryotes (single cell) don't have a gene pool to pass advantages to and from because their "offspring", a daughter cell, is genetically identical (or so we were taught but now that is being contested). It is only in recent years that science has discovered how they rejuvenate to avoid extinction from damage and flaws. Horizontal Gene Transfer (HGT) allows Prokaryotes to repair and share genetic improvements and HGT is surprisingly efficient at doing so. Half of the world's bacterium now share identical drug resistant DNA, and this is true no matter where in the world they have been studied, even in places where man doesn't exist. They draw from the super genome (the DNA available and passed around by individuals in their environment).

Binary fission (cell division) allows prokaryotic life to reproduce, and HGT is a good surrogate for a gene pool. This late research has also discovered that prokaryotes do not evenly distribute the DNA changes they inherit when they divide. Instead, they concentrate most of the changes to just one of the daughter cells. In doing so, they make sure these changes stand the test of Darwinism before they are universally adopted. In addition to this surprising survival strategy, early prokaryotic lifeforms have much more in their bag of tricks.

Prokaryotic life's circular DNA is very different from the nucleic DNA of eukaryotic life, which is the now familiar double helical structure we also possess. Prokaryotes mutated and became our eukaryotic ancestors and then immediately infected them by inserting their prokaryotic DNA into the newly formed eukaryotes. Once inside of our ancestors through endosymbiosis, this ancient code formed the mitochondrion, the part of the cell that fuels cellular functions, and accelerated the evolution of our ancestors. We eukaryotes have the ancient circular DNA of prokaryotes in the mitochondrion of each cell (sometimes thousands of copies per cell). This ancient and non-nucleic DNA has now been proven to influence our behavior.

Evidence linking behavior to mitochondrial DNA comes from the Génétique, Neurogénétique, Comportement Laboratory (genetics, neurogenetics, and behavior) of the CNRS in Orleans, France. From its press release, September 3, 2003 – "Pierre Roubertoux and his team at the CNRS have demonstrated that mice with identical nuclear genomes can have very different cognitive functioning if they do not have the same mitochondria in their cytoplasm. The mitochondria are not transferred with the nucleus during cloning procedures. The results of this research were published in the September issue of the journal Nature Genetics."

The mice of this experiment were cloned and therefore had identical nucleic DNA. This DNA was from the donor cell of one mouse, but the mitochondrial DNA was contributed from the host mouse. It is theorized that this genetic difference is responsible for the noticeable cognitive behavioral differences that exist between the clones and the originals.

More evidence established links between mitochondrial DNA and behavior. Elaine R. Reynolds, Ph.D., Assistant Professor of Developmental Neurobiology and Molecular Genetics at Lafayette College and her team have conducted experiments with flies featuring a mutated mitochondrial DNA. These flies behaved differently than normal flies. The mutant flies had an insensitive reaction to bangs (loud noises) that scared normal flies into flight.

Reynolds' experiment not only reveals the power of mitochondrial mutations over behavior but its potential impact upon survival as well. The insensitive reaction to a potentially life-threatening danger would render flies with this mutation less suited for survival. If important behaviors that help a species survive, like a baby suckling or a honeybee's ability to interpret the hive's communicative dance, were lost then survival for the individual and the entire species would be jeopardized.

The ancient code of earth's first life (prokaryotes) has controlled our evolution and continues to control our lives in remarkable ways. In addition to influencing behavior, the ancient code (via mitochondria) can have a **dramatic impact upon physical properties, and lifespan**. Hybridization exaggerates this control while illustrating it.

Hybridization is the mating of two different but closely related species to produce a viable offspring, though the progeny are normally sterile. One such hybrid, the liger, is a cross between a male lion and a female tiger. The result of this rare breeding produces an animal of gargantuan scale. Its length is about 12 feet long and weighs nearly 1200 pounds or about 75% more than tigers, which are the largest of all non-extinct, naturally occurring big cats.

The Liger

The tigon is also a cross between a tiger and a lion, however, this time the parental roles are reversed, and a lioness is mated with a male tiger. The tigon looks similar in color and markings to the liger, but its size is much smaller than both tigers and lions and completely overshadowed by ligers.

How does the same breeding stock, lions and tigers, produce such dramatically different animals? The mitochondrial DNA.

The genetic differences that create the repeatable and radical difference in size between the liger and tigon are correlated to mother's species because the mitochondrial DNA is contributed by the mother. This mitochondrial mismatch is responsible for these freakish size variations and also shortens the lifespan of ligers and tigons to be significantly less than that of tigers or lions.

Mitochondrial DNA is more important to the species than any one individual's nucleic DNA and therefore must be safeguarded. Changes to this ancient code must move slowly and be continuously tested by natural selection. Prokaryotes, the believed origin of mitochondrial DNA through endosymbiosis, protected this code by concentrating changes to one daughter cell first. If the daughter cell received advantageous differences, it would survive and pass these improvements on. Given the radical changes that can occur by changing the mitochondrial DNA in a species, **eukaryotes needed a way to test these changes through natural selection** first too. Evolution into males and females has created a gene pool that made that possible.

Evolution has dictated that the mothers provide the mitochondrial DNA to the successive generations in the cytoplasm of her eggs and fathers exhibit certain behaviors that in combination will force mitochondrial mutations to be tested by a few in the clan before they would be adopted by the rest and in turn the species.

Early man (or at least the creatures from which we evolved) and many creatures of today's world live in a patriarchal culture. The alpha male fathers the offspring until he is overthrown or dies. If the male supplied the mitochondrial DNA, the future behavior of his clan would be one mutation away from irrevocable change. This change would immediately impact all individuals of the next generation whether it was beneficial to the survival of the clan or not. It would not be tested by natural selection. It would just occur.

To demonstrate the importance the mitochondrial safeguards that natural selection has provided, lets first look at a hypothetical depiction of what would occur if the male were responsible for mitochondrial gene donation. Mutated DNA is depicted with dark fill while the normal mitochondrial DNA is shown with white fill. The circle represents the mating of one male with contemporary generation females of the clan. The individuals outside this circle represent the offspring (next generation) resulting from the mating pairs inside the circle.

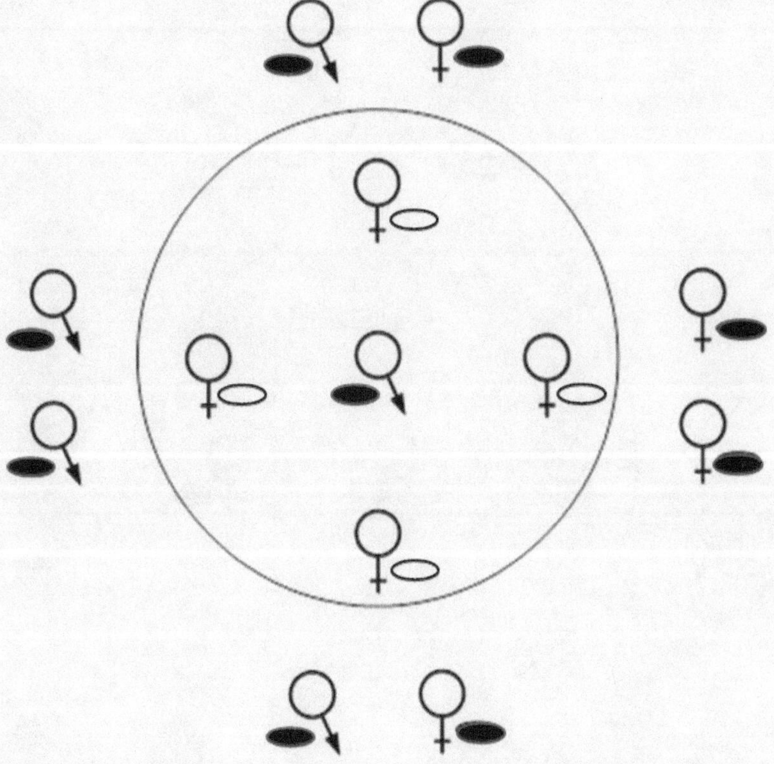

This hypothetic mitochondrial DNA system would result in an immediate change in mitochondrial DNA, impacting every individual in the next generation and all generations to come. This change could adversely impact survival by changing behavior and bodies of the entire next generation. Clearly this would be a dangerous circumstance, as this mutation would not have been tested by natural selection. Given that a male continues to produce sperm throughout their adult life, there are many, many opportunities for mutations to occur during cell division – a dangerous place for the mitochondrial seed to be placed. During the male's life, chance mutations could occur that alter the mitochondrial DNA. This male survived but his descendant's' survivability may be jeopardized.

The following depiction represents the true mitochondrial DNA donation (from the mother).

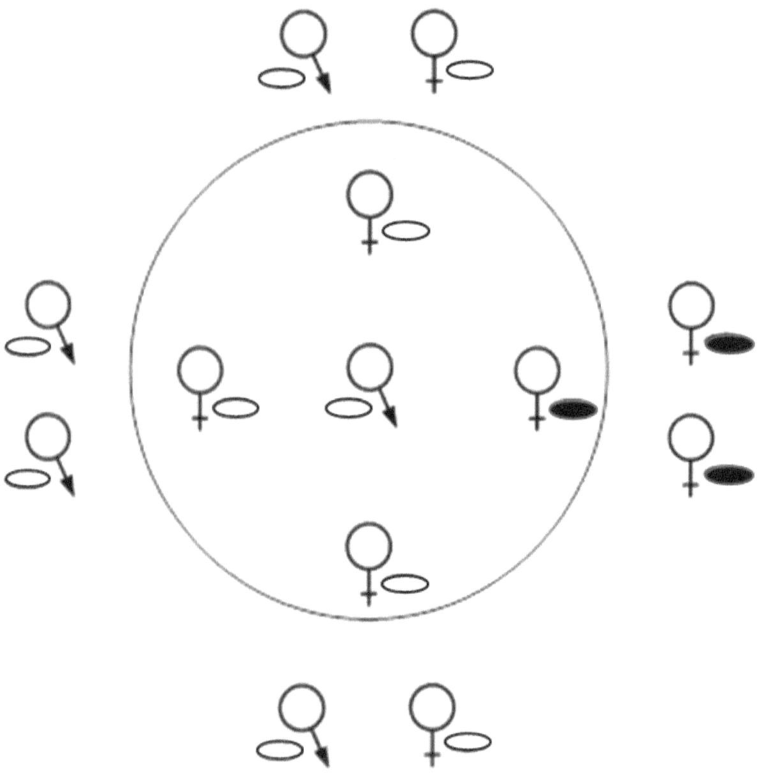

Here, just one female inside the mating circle has mutated mitochondrial DNA. Only her offspring will inherit this mutation, and the balance of this generation's offspring will keep the ancient genetic code. This method ensures that the mutation will have to stand the test of natural selection before the clan completely adopts this change. If the mutation represents improved or same survivability to that of the current code, it will live on. If the mutation is adverse, these individuals and their descendants, if any, will become extinct over time (immediately if the change represents significant impairment).

Mothers are born with a lifetime supply of eggs and as a result, the mitochondrial DNA of the female has far fewer opportunities to mutate, thus protecting the ancient code. **Nature has exercised great care to faithfully replicate the mitochondrial DNA in most, while forcing individual mutations to pass the test of natural selection because the survival of the species depends upon it.**

The bifurcation between nucleic DNA and mitochondrial DNA provides an optimal approach to managing evolutionary change. **The Two Lanes of Evolution**: Mitochondrial DNA, a secure place for species' certain universally important behavioral traits (part of the species' survival strategy) along with the diversity engine of nucleic DNA (also an important part of a species' survival strategy allowing for mutations to overcome changes in the environment and protection against emerging diseases). Together they cooperate to help secure survival of the species.

Prokaryotes can and do test DNA changes via natural selection by limiting its transfer to just a select few individuals at first. This ancient code became the mitochondrial DNA of eukaryotes and through its influence upon the size, body structure and behavior of us eukaryotes, maintains test by natural selection of this life-governing ancient code, despite it being present in the multicellular eukaryotes' gene pool (diversity engine).

Man's Clumsy Approach Has Revealed Life Expectancy can be Manipulated

Mankind plays faster and looser with genetic change than nature and thus can produce significant deviations more quickly. Sheep and cattle and other mammals have now been cloned. These mammalian clones by definition are genetically identical (nucleic) to the donor, yet some clones aged at a different rate than the original organism. Some of the clones have aged significantly faster, while others have aged much slower than the original. As soon as we attempted to bypass natural selection, we altered the number of acts in the play of life.

Cloned organisms that aged at an unexpected rate did so because the genes selected for cloning came from somatic cells with a diploid (complete compliment of genes necessary for life) chromosome count and not gametes (sperm and ova) which have only half the genes necessary for life (haploid). Some of the somatic cells selected had already begun the aging process (in the middle of the Hayflick limit) and as a result had less telomere length than normally present at conception. The shortened telomeres gave rise to a clone with a shortened lifespan. Normally, the source of DNA for the fertilized egg is the egg itself and a sperm cell, which fertilizes it. Each contributes half the nucleic DNA required for life with normal telomere length. Therefore, normal egg fertilization arises from DNA material that isn't subjected to the shortened telomeres that comes from aged somatic cells.

DNA used in cloning, from prepubescent donors, produces an egg with enhanced telomere/TM replication capabilities because the DNA originates from cells that still have the self-replication via TM switched on. This enhancement yields an organism with extraordinary lifespan potential.

The Massachusetts based company, Advanced Cell Technology (ACT), has slowed the aging process in six cloned cows. The clones appear to possess cells that are younger than the cells of normal cows of the same age. The clones originated from in vitro aged fetal cells. Their research indicates that animals cloned from cells with restored telomeres possess telomeres that are even longer than newborn cows reproduced through normal procreation. This suggested that cloning could expand the lifespan of cells and the multicellular organism that contains those cells.

Dr. Xiangzhong (Jerry) Yang, Professor in the Department of Animal Science and Head of the Transgenic Animal Facility at the University of Connecticut Biotechnology Center said, "They (ACT scientists) found that their fetal clones had longer telomeres than aged-matched control (cows) whereas we found normal telomere lengths in our adult-derived clones," said Yang. "The differences are likely due to different sources of the donor cells (fetus vs. adult) and different culture conditions. The donor cells in our study were cultured only briefly whereas those in the ACT study were cultured to near senescence (termination of cell division capability). Over-compensation in telomere reprogramming is a possibility when near-senescent cells were used for cloning because they are near the limit of telomere shortening." This behavior is remarkably similar to the conjugative response of paramecia when near the Hayflick Limit.

Mankind's attempts at cloning have revealed that the gears of a species' biological clock are fragile and easily shifted. This distortion is not really because we know what we are doing. It is instead because aging is like an intricately engineered and delicate watch. It doesn't take a hammer very well.

Cancer cells do not have a Hayflick Limit. They continue to divide and grow indefinitely until they are either stopped or kill the host. Keeping in mind that life is virile enough to survive in a variety of extreme environments; it is surprising that "normal" cells die just because they have lived while chance mutations immediately become immortal. This strongly suggests that **normal cells are programmed to die.** The program to die is a dead end that blocks only one lane of the Two Lanes of Evolution – the nucleic DNA, the part that makes you unique. Nature wants you to disappear once you have done your job. The other lane is for the ancient code of life, contained in our mitochondrion and representative of the entire species, is intended to go on forever. This lane has no end.

Religion

I have restricted the references to religion to just this section. Those who are interested in only the biological facts may bypass them and therefore avoid what religious bias I may bring. I have included these observations for completeness and to enable the reader to identify any false conclusions I may have unintentionally reached due to my perspective.

The "religious" among sometimes reject evolutionary theory and sometimes personally attack Charles Darwin. On occasion, evolutionists also personally attack creationists. Evidence of a clash between creationists and evolutionists can be seen playing out on the bumpers of cars across America. Some persons have adorned their car with a symbol of faith:

This emblem should not create controversy yet some have made a passive, aggressive response to it and placed the following emblem on their car's bumper:

While creative and an example of the evolution of automotive adornment, it is somewhat impolite and disrespectful. Not be outdone, offended creationists have countered back with:

The battle of bumpers has proven to have abrasive folks on both sides of the issue. In my opinion, the last image got it right – the TRUTH does contain evolution – though I am sure the designer did intend for me to reach this conclusion. By studying and embracing Darwin's work, we are left with a firm understanding of evolution (origin of species). The fit is great and supported by a wealth of evidence.

Genetic heritage has been found in multi-cellular life forms. Beyond the obvious prokaryote/eukaryote relationship, researchers have proven that birds still contain the genes of their dinosaur past. Changes in the normal timing of activation of the genes of chickens can cause the developing embryo to grow scales, teeth and a tail. These genes were not introduced to the chicken by the researchers. Instead, they were always there. The researchers just changed the sequence of their activation. I'm not certain how creationists can rationalize these facts.

Evolution is the mechanism responsible for the creation of the world's past, present and future species. **Darwin's theory propels a very accurate understanding of the origin of species but not the origin of life**

or death. Evolution provides no answers or scientific explanation for the origin of life and death. This is not because Darwin's work is unfinished but rather because evolution has no application here. The domain of evolution resides between the boundaries of life and death and no further. In this way, Darwin does not have to be the threat to creationists that is first suspected. The traditional evolutionary context maintains that organisms, which more recently evolved, are further improved and therefore more complex than earlier creatures on the evolutionary path. What if that very first cell was in fact more complex than all life that followed? It's time to look past mans' distorted, self-recognized importance and see life for what it is. On with it!

Death does not Exist; it is Folklore

The Ship of Theseus paradox: If, over time, this ship is repaired and maintained by replacing its planks, one board at a time until eventually the entire ship has been replaced, are you left with a new ship or is it still the ship of Theseus? If you add a passenger to this ship it becomes a fitting metaphor for life.

It is striking that our very first eukaryotic ancestor immediately sacrificed the bit of itself that was old (the paramecium's ejection of the macronucleus) so soon after rejuvenation was achieved. **This disregard for the part of life that has already served its purpose to ensure the species' survival and is no longer needed would eventually evolve into our view of death.** Paramecia and other single cell eukaryotes found a way past death due to aging. They survived and went onto create multicellular life and accelerate evolution. One of these multicellular descendants is man. The result of the evolution into the sexes provides a mechanism to reset the Hayflick Limit with each successive generation. For multicellular organisms, becoming young again is limited to just the offspring. The parents, having done their job to ensure survival of the species, wither and die for all but a few lucky species. **We are analogous to and descendants of the old, disintegrating macronucleus of paramecia.** We are the evolved body parts of our ancestral past. Only the part containing the circular DNA of our ancestors remains immortal.

In the first paragraph I asked, why does life succumb to death just because it has lived? Given that all species evolved from ageless life, it is paradoxical that the more "complex" lifeforms that followed could not continue to live. Truly, evolution is a mistake rich process. **Life is composed of single cell organisms and death is comprised of multicellular organisms.**

We don't think a caterpillar dies when it transforms into a butterfly. We understand it as the next stage in the life of the species. Likewise, we didn't view death for the paramecium when it became its own offspring; but we do recognize death of humans. Why?

Our individual consciousness and our memories are contained outside of the immortal part of us. It is in the region that will age, wither and die. This is what causes us to believe that we will die when the organism that began it all, the ageless prokaryote, continues to live on by disembarking from one ship (body) and boarding the next just as nature intended. We are already ageless. Most would prefer that the part that is not ageless (our bodies and minds) could continue with the rest of the journey.

Contained in women's eggs is the ancient prokaryotic code for life. Our bodies protect and replicate them. The cellular path from the single egg that produced our mother to the egg she used to grow us is remarkably short. The eggs reproduce themselves very quickly after fertilization indicating that human existence is a consequence of service to the conception of the next generation. Her body provides this single cell organism a means to continue, stepping out of her body and into the body of her child. Her body and mind develop to ensure survival long enough to repeat the cycle of life.

When viewing human existence this way males, females, our desires and dreams are reduced to just the evolved survival strategies in service the original, immortal cells of life. This would tend to answer the question, "what came first, the chicken or the egg?" The egg did. For man, it is a single cell organism that over time evolved an intricate cocoon for the origin of life that we know as ourselves.

The evolutionary process of natural selection is normally viewed as a mechanism that produces more advanced standalone lifeforms over time. Instead, it creates more advanced and more diverse cocoons to protect the relatively unchanging original lifeform. This view reveals a layer of continuity that is normally overlooked. **Our bodies are the Ship of Theseus**. Our bodies are a type of vessel, one form among many (deer, fish, plants past and present). They ensure the survival of the ancient cells of life. The part of humans that is ageless is the ancient, cocooned, **prokaryotic passengers** contained in the cytoplasm of our species' and their voyage continues uninterrupted from one ship to the next. The Ship of Theseus is a new ship. In fact, it is just one of millions of ships that have been replaced for the last 2 billion years. The new planks contain subtle, imperceptible improvements within their cells that continue to adapt to the changing waters they encounter. The old planks (multicellular organisms) have been cast off for millenniums, piling up and compressing into fossils. Over billions of years both the layer of fossils and advancements (mutations to the vessel) have piled up impressively while the passengers have barely changed.

We view humans as individuals though we are part of the same gigantic organism. An individual of a species is like a hand to a body. If the hand was lost, the individual lives on and we do not call it death. Likewise, the loss of an individual in the service of life's continuum is not death but a survival mechanism.

If the continuance of life allowed our consciousness to convey to our offspring, we would tend to view the ejection of a spent, lifeless body as a transition from one phase of life to the next, and no longer recognize this process as death. **It is our ego that dies and not our life.** Our individual thoughts, beliefs and memories are unimportant to the continuum of life.

My father used to tell me that mankind was the only organism on the planet that noticed the great depression. The sky was still blue, the grass remained green and the birds still chirped. Our ego can force us to imagine a lot. Death is a manmade notion. Life is a continuum.